HOLIDAY FUN!
FOURTH OF JULY

by Lily Austen

TABLE OF CONTENTS

Words to Know 2

Fourth of July 3

Let's Review! 16

Index 16

WORDS TO KNOW

colors

fireworks

flags

parade

sparklers

wave

FOURTH OF JULY

It is July 4!

We wear colors.

Red, white, and blue.

We wave flags.

We eat food.

We see a parade.

We see sparklers.

We see fireworks.

Fun!

LET'S REVIEW!

The Fourth of July celebrates the United States' freedom. How is this family celebrating?

INDEX

colors 4
fireworks 14
flags 7

food 9
parade 11
sparklers 13